Bad Haiku for Drummers

David Aron

ISBN: 1-7344091-0-X

ISBN-13: 978-1-7344091-0-9

Some characters and events in this book are fictitious. Any similarity to real persons, living or dead, is coincidental and not intended by the author.

Books may be purchased by contacting the publisher:

Whyze Group
2233 S. Overlook Rd.
Cleveland, Ohio, USA 44106
jason@whyzegroup.com

ACKNOWLEDGMENTS

If you have bad haiku that you'd like to share with drummers worldwide, please email it to the publisher, Whyze Group, at jason@whyzegroup.com. If your submission is included in updates of *Bad Haiku for Drummers*, your contribution will be acknowledged here. Thank you! We sincerely hope you enjoy this book.

BAD HAIKU FOR DRUMMERS

INTRODUCTION

Welcome to *Bad Haiku for Drummers!* This fun gift is delighting drummers of every level.

It's based on my twenty-five years of experience learning and playing drums with rock bands, jazz ensembles and musical theatre productions. Many pages summarize common-sense tips shared by some of the best drummers of all time.

This is also the world's first *greeting book*--for when a greeting card isn't enough. A card lasts ten seconds, but this greeting book gives you or your favorite drummer *five whole minutes* of drummer haiku insight and joy.

So, get ready for bad haiku. I've definitely earned an F on my haiku writing here. The good thing is drummers who've read this say it was the most thoughtful, entertaining few minutes they've spent this week.

I hope you'll enjoy it, too.

-David Aron, Author

HAIKU OF

LEARNING TO PLAY DRUMS LIKE A BOSS

Learn about
independence—
four limbs playing
four different rhythms
on four different instruments.

Mastering it
will be more impressive than
learning calculus.

Be nice, play well and be humble.
You can always be replaced
by a button
on a drum machine.

You'll learn that a paradiddle is
an important drum rudiment.

And, a flam-para-diddle-diddle is
a form of
medieval torture.

If God just wanted
you to make loud noise,
She'd have made drum sets
less expensive
than practice pads.

After spending two months learning
the double-stroke roll
with your hands,
you'll spend two years learning
how to do it with your feet.

Someday, this will make sense:

4 sixteenth notes, followed by
3 thirty-second notes,
1 thirty-second note rest,
1 sixteenth note rest and
1 sixteenth note.

Playing a drum set in school.
You'll become the object
of puppy love
even if you still feel
like a geek.

During your first 10,000 hours
of practice on a drum set
you can make a small income
selling ear plugs to your neighbors.

Sheet music is
our written language.
Reading it is less annoying to your bandmates
than constantly asking them
what to play.

At least a third of your practice time
should be with a metronome.
Yup, you actually have to turn it on
and play with the darn thing.

Loud drumming
isn't always good.
Good drumming is
always good.
Sometimes it's loud.

You'll learn that jamming
with bassoon players
isn't all
it's cracked up to be.

As a drummer in
your first garage band,
you'll see why you'll never
play loud enough
for guitar players.

(Bring ear plugs.)

Auditions for singers
in your first garage band
will include nice people
who are exceptional
caterwaulers.

Learn to play every genre
but remember:
if you can play rock,
you might have a
better-than-even chance
of getting paid.

...Some day.

Protect your hearing.

When you buy
noise cancelling earphones
you'll appreciate that the noise
you're cancelling
is you.

HAIKU OF

TURNING PRO

In your first rehearsal
with real professionals,
you'll think,
"I've got this."

…until they pull out
a chart
in 11/8 time.

The math of becoming a pro
made sense before
you had to buy
a $20,000 gig van
to move your $3,500 drum set.

Be prepared for anything
when gigging.
Bring extra sticks, drum keys,
drum heads, underwear
and wrenches.

Just kidding about
the underwear.

Lucky you!
You've got your
first paid gig.

Now, roadie your
eleven-piece drum set
up those stairs.

If the venue has a drum kit,
then you'll only need to bring
your cymbals, pedals,
sticks and extra stands.

Congratulations.

You're carrying only
fifty pounds of gear now.

After years of
tuning drums,
you'll realize that
there's always one lug
on one drum
that goes
p-i-i-i-ng, boink or thud
no matter how
you tune it.

The chance that your
bass drum pedal
will break during a performance
is directly proportional to:

How much you're getting paid
for the gig,
or how soon
your drum solo is.

You'll be feeling great about
your sixteenth note grooves
until sixteenth note *quintuplets*
become trendy.

"More cowbell"
pleases audiences
more than
anything else.

And, you only
have to say it.

Prepare for encores.

No matter whether
you're performing
jazz, fusion or musical theater,
there will always be someone
at the end of a gig
who shouts,
"Free Bird."

Note from the Author

Thank you for reading *Bad Haiku for Drummers*. Whatever occasion you're celebrating, I hope this book has added five minutes of unbridled joy to it!

If you've enjoyed *Bad Haiku for Drummers*, I hope you'll write a review on Amazon or wherever you bought this book. It really helps support my bad haiku writing.

Thanks again,

David Aron

www.ingramcontent.com/pod-product-compliance
Lightning Source LLC
Chambersburg PA
CBHW031635040426
42452CB00007B/841